The Nature of Risk

In the *Nature of Risk*, David X Martin uses an easily understood fable to explain the often overlooked and misunderstood concepts of risk management, simplifying them into clear messages for all audiences. Readers are sure to appreciate the lessons learned from this unique tale.

Ajay Banga
CEO, MasterCard

A charming and deceptively powerful primer on risk. One comes away from this quick read with a renewed commitment to pay attention to what is going on around you, and to make conscious decisions on how to protect what is important to you.

Bill Wyman
Co-founder, Oliver Wyman

David Martin's fable, *The Nature of Risk*, provides a unique perspective on the challenges and opportunities of risk taking. Most texts on this subject are either histories of financial disasters or highly technical, and focus on mathematical techniques. Martin's little book, on the other hand, creates a beautiful tale of animals in a forest and their reactions (or lack thereof) to a range of natural catastrophes. That alone makes it a rare and valuable contribution. However, Martin also makes an additional contribution to the equation-laden risk literature by highlighting that different individuals have different risk "personalities" that predispose them to different vulnerabilities. In contrast, many more "sophisticated" treatises neglect this basic fact. Only a seasoned risk professional like Martin would recognize the importance of this often overlooked insight. After all, how else can it be that so many giant financial entities have been brought down by such a small handful of employees?

Bennett Golub
Founding Partner/Chief Risk Officer, Blackrock

David Martin has produced a rich parable of risk management for our troubled times. In a crisp and accessible narrative, part children's story and part handbook, Martin's wisdom and experience shine through. He has provided the perfect rebuttal to those who mistakenly imagine that risk management has nothing to do with real life.

Michael Power
Director of the Centre for the Analysis of
Risk and Regulation,
London School of Economics

In the same way that one of our greatest film makers has recently taken a children's story and turned it into a spectacular, adult-themed war movie, David X Martin has taken the complex, adult issues involved with managing risk and turned them into a simple fable anyone can understand and enjoy.

But a children's book this isn't. By showing us the various ways that forest-dwelling animals face up to and deal with risk, Martin succeeds in showing us how we manage risk ourselves. *The Nature of Risk* is a quick read, but it's also a thoughtful approach to a complex subject, and Martin handles that complexity with the same ease that successful children's authors tell their stories.

Jerry Lieberman
Former President, AllianceBernstein

Over thirty years of successful investing has taught me that the most important starting point is "Know Thyself". Without this knowledge, one can only be a gambler swayed by headlines and sales pitches. With it, one can conquer the fear of risk as well as the lure of greed and make rational decisions that pay off in the long run. I recommend David X Martin's book not only to the novice investor but also to the most sophisticated one. It offers a rare dose of common sense, insight, and wisdom that will benefit every reader.

G. Lynn Shostack
President, Gardner Capital Corp.

With *The Nature of Risk* David X Martin has done what countless others have tried and failed to do—that is, make the basics of risk management not only easy to understand, but entertaining too.

William R. Rhodes
Former Senior Vice Chairman, Citigroup
Author of *Banker to the World* (McGraw-Hill 2011)

By using the simple but powerful metaphor of forest animals facing risks in their habitat, David Martin has made the essentials of risk management accessible to everyone. There are lessons here for all audiences, from families managing their personal finances to professionals setting risk management strategies in complex enterprises. A key lesson in the fable is that "zero risk" is unattainable, and that taking some risk proactively is an important part of risk management in both our personal and professional lives.

John Drzik
CEO, Oliver Wyman Group

THE NATURE OF RISK

Are you a bear, a squirrel, a turtle, or a fox?

By

David X Martin

For my wife, Barbara, on whose shoulders I stand.

Introduction

I wrote this book for those of you who believe it's still possible to make sense of the world we live in. If you're one of those people, this book is meant to offer you hope. Hope that you *can* arrive at some basic understanding of the way certain things work, and then take some sort of meaningful action, given your goals. But like so many stories of hope, this one begins with a moment of great sadness.

A few years ago one of my closest friends collapsed without warning, and died before the paramedics could get him to the hospital. Everyone who knew him was devastated. He was still in the prime of his life. He was well respected in the community. He had a large family, a lot of friends, and a successful business. But he was gone, just like that, and there was nothing anybody could do about it.

A few weeks later his widow asked me if I'd be willing to help her sort out the family's finances. Her late husband had always taken care of the money, she said, and she was confused by all the different accounts. I agreed to help, of course, and a couple nights later I started looking over the family's books. Before long I could see that, while he'd been a good businessman, my late friend hadn't been much of a risk manager. His retirement account, for instance, was not only woefully under-funded, it was all in short-term CDs that paid less interest than the current rate of inflation. The opposite was true of his kids' college funds. His two youngest children, twin boys who were then seniors in high school, had a good amount of money in their names, but unlike their parents' retirement account, every penny of it was invested in highly volatile stocks.

Nor were the risks limited to investments. My friend's eldest daughter had married the year before, and she and her husband had moved into an apartment in the city. He owned a small computer software company, and she was an account-ant. Turning through a folder I saw that my friend and his wife had recently cosigned the young couple's application for a mortgage. There was a sales contract in the folder, too, for a three-bedroom apartment in the city, with a closing date only a few weeks off. From what I could see, his daughter and her husband had saved some money, but only enough for the down payment—which meant that if they spent it all on the apartment they'd have no cushion left. To further complicate matters, my friend's daughter was four months pregnant.

When I spoke to them on the phone, it turned out that buying an apartment was my friend's daughter's idea. Her husband, to put it plainly, didn't want to take the risk. For starters, he was worried about his company's future. If he had to forgo his salary for a few months, he wasn't sure they'd be able to pay the mortgage—especially when his wife took time off to have the baby. She reminded him that they were going to hire a nanny so she could keep working, and if his company ran into trouble he could always find another job, couldn't he? Besides, she said, you can't go through life worrying about everything that *might* go wrong. If they had to sell the apartment, they'd still get their down payment back, wouldn't they? But if they kept paying rent, they'd just be throwing their money away.

I asked the husband a few questions about his company. Did they specialize in a particular kind of software? Yes, they did: project management. And how were sales? Still strong, he said. But while the company had grown quickly over the past five years, he'd just gotten word that one of the biggest players in the industry was coming out with a product that would go head-to-head with his company's best seller. And he and his management team were having trouble deciding whether they should concentrate on supporting the product they already had on the market, or start looking for another niche —while they still had time.

Over the next few days my thoughts kept circling back to the various risks faced by my friend's family. His wife's retirement account was so conservatively invested that if she lived past the age of seventy-five she'd probably run out of money. And what about his daughter's insistence that she and her husband should buy an apartment? The real estate market had been surging for years, which made me question their timing. Plus, she was pregnant, and buying the apartment now meant they'd exhaust their savings at a time when their cash flow was uncertain. Then there was the young husband's software company. Was it a bigger risk to stick with the established product they had, and battle a much larger competitor? Or was the biggest risk trying to develop a new product—for a market that didn't even exist yet? Finally, there were the twins' college accounts, which their mother would need in a little over nine months, and which were invested so aggressively that a downturn in the stock market might make it necessary to borrow money for their educations.

* * *

I knew right away what I'd do in each of these situations. I'd been a professional risk manager most of my adult life, and for me these sorts of decisions were almost automatic. Why? Because I knew the sort of risks I was willing to take to reach my goals, and how to balance risk and reward. But this wasn't my money, and I didn't want to *tell* my friend's family what to do. Instead, I wanted to teach them a few simple, fundamental principles of risk management, and then encourage each of them to create a *process* for managing risk—a process they'd be able to use for the rest of their lives, no matter what they were doing, and no matter how their goals changed. And in that way, I thought, perhaps some small, lasting good might come of my friend's death.

But it was easier said than done.

Not one of them wanted to learn anything about risk management. Instead, they just wanted me to make their decisions for them, and let them get on with their lives. I was the risk manager, wasn't I? So manage their risks, they said, and let them get back to doing what they did. I tried to convince them that it wasn't that hard to learn the basics, and more importantly, that no one knew their risk appetites as well as they did. I told them that if they did nothing more than consider the risks they faced, they'd sleep better at night. But it was almost as if they believed that thinking about risk management was in itself some kind of risk.

So in the end I caved in. I rebalanced the wife's retirement portfolio and the twins' college accounts. As for the apartment, I didn't take sides. I just told the young couple they had to sit down together and ask themselves how much they were willing to risk to own a place of their own, keeping in mind that prices had been rising for years, that home ownership implied certain additional costs, and that there was no *guarantee* they'd be able to sell the apartment for what they paid.

I gave my friend's son-in-law the same advice regarding his company. He had to start by assessing his company's health, and then asking himself what his goals were. Did he want to grow the company, or was he content to run a small business? If he was happy where he was, what did he think his company's chances were of surviving a battle with a much larger competitor? Had he considered selling the company? If he didn't want to sell, had he considered the *advantages* he enjoyed as the head of a smaller enterprise? His company had the ability to turn on a dime, without lengthy discussions or approvals, and if what he said about his workforce was true, they all seemed willing and capable of trying something new. In the end, though, he had to make the decision himself.

* * *

A few months went by, and every time I checked in with my friend's wife, I couldn't help thinking about my own family. What would my wife and children do if I weren't around to continually reassess the risks of modern life, and manage them accordingly?

So one night, after the dinner dishes had been cleared, I asked everyone to sit back down at the table. Once they were seated, I told them I was going to teach them the basics of risk management. They sat there like I'd turned them to stone. I launched into my speech anyway, because unlike my friend's family, they *had* to listen to me. Within five minutes, however, it became clear that teaching my wife and children about risk management was going to be about as easy as reducing the national debt. So I let them go.

But I couldn't get it out of my mind. Why was it so hard to get people to start thinking about risk? Just to think about it, before they made the decisions that would lead either to success or failure? There had to be a way. And so, after a few weeks' thought I settled on a different approach. Borrowing a page from some of the best communicators in the business—the authors of children's books—I decided I'd write a simple story. A simple, memorable, and entertaining story that would make thinking about risk, and what one can do about it, easier for anyone who had the good luck to read it.

* * *

After a little more thought, I decided to set the story in the forests north of New York City, where I had spent time as a boy. The story's main characters would be a red squirrel, a rabbit, a rat snake, a woodpecker, a gray squirrel, a turtle, a herd of white-tailed deer, a red fox, and a colony of beavers. Each animal, or group of animals, has its own way of managing risk, and those approaches are put to the test by two pivotal events—a brush fire, and a forest fire.

As it turned out, setting this story in the forest meant that I had less work to do than I thought. In fact, a lot of the story wrote itself, since the animals' instinctual approaches to survival—the ultimate form of risk management—mirror the way a lot of us deal with risk. Some of the animals, for instance, mistakenly believe that they can simply avoid risk. Some merely run with the herd. Others are oblivious to the risks around them. Still others change their approach so often that they really don't have an approach at all.

As you read the story, my guess is that you'll see an animal that resembles you—that is, an animal that deals with risks the way you do. You'll see parallels, too, in the way *groups* of animals approach risk, and can compare the behavior of those groups to the collective actions of men and women in any organization, large or small. Finally, once you've finished the story, you'll come to a short point-by-point review designed to help you start putting what you've learned about risk management, and about yourself, to work.

That said, I hope you'll turn the next fifty pages for the same reason you turn the pages of any good book—because you can't wait to find out how the story ends.

Author's Note:
While no animals were intentionally
harmed in the telling of this story,
a number of them will be unavailable
for the sequel.

The Forest

This story began in the heart of a great forest, where the mountains to the north gave way to a series of gently sloping valleys, and where the lakes were too small and inaccessible to have been given names. A stream wound its way down the middle of one of these valleys, cutting right and left through the trees, splashing over the rocks and pebbles in its path, and finally pouring out into a large pond. Beavers swam across the pond, sending V-shaped ripples through the water. On the far side of the pond was a jagged dam made of mud and branches, and below the dam was a meadow, its grass swaying in the breeze.

The sun hung just above the pine trees along the western ridge, and to the east the silvery leaves of a stand of aspen fluttered in the last light of the day. As the daylight faded, birds darted across the evening sky, squirrels rustled through the trees, and small animals scampered across the forest floor.

At the edge of the meadow stood a massive oak tree, and a fat red squirrel sat on one of its lowest branches. Looking out across the meadow he saw a cottontail bounding through the grass. As the rabbit came closer, the red squirrel leaned forward and called down to him.

"Hey, rabbit. What's the hurry?"

The rabbit stopped and peered up at the squirrel.

"What's the hurry? Are you blind, squirrel? There are coyotes and foxes everywhere, and hawks, too," said the rabbit, glancing nervously up into the sky. "If you don't keep moving, something'll be on your trail before you know it."

The red squirrel yawned.

"So what? That doesn't mean you have to run around until you collapse, does it? Can't you just find yourself a nice safe place to hang out? You know, so you wouldn't have to worry every minute of your life."

The rabbit cleaned his whiskers with his forepaws.

"I can't take that risk, squirrel."

"What risk? Look at me. I've lived in this oak tree for years, and I've got so many acorns stuffed into the thing I'll never go hungry again. If you weren't in such a rush all the time, you could learn something from a squirrel like me."

"Yeah? Like what?" said the rabbit. "Sitting in one place all day and eating acorns makes you too fat to run?"

The red squirrel scratched his head.

"Run? Who needs to run? I've got everything I need right here," he said, extending one tiny paw in the direction of the tree trunk.

"Everything to *lose* is more like it."

And with that, the rabbit hopped back into the grass and out of sight. As the squirrel watched the rabbit go, he heard something else on the ground beneath him, and leaning forward, he saw a black rat snake looking up at him, its tail coiled neatly beneath it.

"*Sssalutations*, squirrel. Couldn't help hearing you tell that rabbit that you had a *nice* pile of acorns tucked away up there," said the snake, drawing out the word *nice* until it really didn't sound very nice at all.

The red squirrel frowned.

"What's it to you, snake?"

"Just looking to offer my *ssservices*," said the snake, looking first to the right, and then to the left, and then up at the red squirrel again.

"And what services would those be?" asked the red squirrel.

"*Sssurveillance*, squirrel."

"What?"

"I…how should I put it? I keep an eye on things."

"So do I," said the red squirrel, crossing his paws on chest. "So what do I need you for?"

"Oh, we can all use a little help, squirrel. After all, acorns don't *lassst* forever. Bugs get into them, rainwater makes them rot, and other animals *sssteal* them behind your back."

The red squirrel shrugged.

"Tell me something I don't know, snake."

The snake's forked tongue flicked hungrily over the tiny sharp teeth that lined his jaws.

"I'm only looking to help, squirrel," said the snake, beginning to slither away from the oak. "But just remember *thisss*. Those acorns won't *lassst* forever." His words fading to a whisper, the rat snake disappeared into the grass; in a hurry, it seemed, to be on his way.

A moment later a magnificently colored woodpecker flew

through the trees and, spreading his broad black and white wings wide, dropped onto a branch across from the red squirrel.

"Hope you're smart enough to think twice before you do business with that snake," said the woodpecker, beginning to preen his feathers with his long pointed beak.

"Plenty smart enough," said the squirrel, admiring the woodpecker's bright red cap, "even if he is right about me losing a few acorns every now and then. But who cares? This oak tree is as solid as a rock, and I've got so much to eat here I'll never run out."

The woodpecker tucked his wings tight and hopped up the tree trunk. Gripping the bark tightly, he started to probe it with his beak, looking as comfortable on the side of the tree as he would have if he were perched on a branch.

"You're not the first animal to say that," said the wood-pecker. "But for what it's worth, it's always a good idea to remind yourself that things can change pretty quickly in the forest."

"What's that supposed to mean?"

"Just this. You wouldn't be the first animal to say you were all set for the winter, and then a couple months later find your-self on the ground, searching for nuts under the snow."

And then, with a single mighty flap of his wings, he was gone.

Farther up the valley, a black bear rambled down the stream, pausing to disturb a rock or a tree branch every so often. His noisy approach had already sent the smaller animals in the area into hiding. Mice had disappeared into their burrows, chipmunks had scurried into their tunnels beneath the leaves and twigs, and a gray squirrel, after a quick look at the approaching bear, had hurried up a tree trunk until she was high above the ground.

Unlike the red squirrel, the gray squirrel had nuts and seeds stockpiled throughout the forest. That way, if another animal got into one of her nests, or a bear kept her from getting to another, she could always head toward a third, or a fourth, or a fifth. And as the black bear wandered along the forest floor, that's just what she did, quickly leaving the bear behind.

Hearing the leaves rustle above him, the black bear paused and glanced up. The woodpecker was perched on the lower-most branch of the swamp maple just over his head.

"Good evening, bear."

"Woodpecker."

His curiosity satisfied, the bear started moving again, and the woodpecker had to hop along the branch to keep up with him.

"You're headed in the right direction, bear…that is, if you don't want to cross paths with that hunting party coming over the eastern ridge."

"Don't care if I do, don't care if I don't," said the bear, raking a bush with one paw to look for berries, and then continuing on. Above him, the woodpecker reached the end

of the branch.

"Your call, bear, but with all due respect, I've seen hunters carry bigger skins than yours out of the forest."

"I'll risk it," said the bear, lumbering off as a distant gunshot echoed through the valley.

"Doesn't matter how big you are, bear," the woodpecker called out. "You can't avoid risk…all you can do is choose the risks you want to take!"

* * *

The fat red squirrel watched the bear lumber off into the woods, and as he did he saw something out of the corner of his eye. Twisting around and looking down, he could just make out the rabbit, lying almost motionless in the brown grass at the edge of the meadow.

"Hey, rabbit," he called out. "What're you doing down there? I thought you said you were going to keep moving?"

The rabbit raised his ears, looked around until he was sure the bear was out of range, and then hopped out of the grass.

"Why don't you shut up, you dumb squirrel? Can't you see when a guy's trying to hide?"

The squirrel put his paws in the air.

"Sorry, rabbit, but what happened to keeping on the move?"

"I'm worn out, that's what happened. Know any good places to hide?"

* * *

Downwind, a herd of deer grazed in a small clearing in the woods. A buck with widespread antlers stood on the highest point, lifting his nose every so often and swiveling his ears.

The woodpecker flew over the herd, then wheeled around and found a perch in the highest branches of a dead ash tree. As the deer grazed below him the woodpecker probed the tree, hopping from branch to branch, pecking at the smooth gray wood and looking for any signs of insects. After a while, finding nothing to his liking, he jumped down to one of the lowest branches and called out to the buck.

"Hello, down there."

The buck looked up slowly, and then gave the woodpecker a majestic nod, his rack spread out above his head like a crown.

"I've got a little news to pass along," said the woodpecker. "There's a bear in the valley, and a pack of coyotes, too."

The deer's antlers again dipped slightly in acknowledgment, and after chewing his cud a while longer, he spoke.

"I know, but they aren't close enough to worry me."

The woodpecker nodded, and began to preen his feathers.

"What about the hunters? Did you hear that rifle shot?"

The buck cocked his head, as if listening for an echo, and then shrugged his massive shoulders.

"I didn't."

"Well, they can't be the only ones out there, so you might think about putting someone else on watch."

The buck snorted.

"The herd follows me, and me only."

And as if to make his point, he raised one hoof in the air and then stomped it on the ground. Every deer in the herd raised its head. The buck gave the woodpecker a withering look, his demonstration complete, and then lowered his antlers and began to feed again.

To the west, a red fox trotted over the ridge and headed down toward the meadow. She hadn't been out of her burrow more than fifteen minutes, and she already had a vole in her teeth. Of course, she too had caught the scent of coyote as soon as she poked her nose out of her burrow, but unlike the other animals, she didn't turn tail and run—she made straight for the pack. Coyotes weren't the kind of animals you wanted to play around with, especially when they were hunting together, but they could come in handy if you knew what you were doing. Like all the big predators, they forced small game out into the open. So if you stayed close, but not so close that you risked being eaten yourself, a pack of coyotes would almost always send a few small animals your way. Now, with the vole's limp body between her teeth, the she-fox picked her way cautiously through the trees until she came to the edge of the meadow.

With her nose in the air and her ears erect, she paused just short of the grass. She never approached either of the entrances to her den—or the exits, depending on which way you looked at it—until she was sure that *both* of them were clear. She and her mate had a few other burrows nearby, and kept a little food in them, too, just in case. But as the sun sank that afternoon their cubs were piled one on top of the other in the big den beneath the meadow. And since it was almost dinnertime, she took one last look around and then trotted out into the meadow.

* * *

Farther east, on the leaf-strewn ground beneath the aspens, a young beaver waddled from tree to tree. Finally coming to one that suited him, he rose up on his hind legs, put his forefeet against the trunk, braced himself with his tail, and sank his teeth into the soft wood. Moving methodically around the tree, he gnawed at the trunk with his sharp incisors, creating a ring of wood chips on the ground beneath him. Then, when the crown of the tree began to shake, he dropped down onto all fours and scuttled backward. At first the aspen swayed like a camper who'd had too many beers, but after reaching out to the other trees in a vain attempt to stay on its feet, it finally toppled to the ground. Before its leaves had stopped shaking, an older beaver appeared and headed for the downed tree, while another young member of the colony stopped to talk to the beaver that had just sent the tree crashing to the ground.

"Pssst," he whispered, "don't you think we're taking too big a risk cutting trees down out here? There are coyotes in the valley, and look how far away from the pond we are."

The older, silver-furred beaver, overhearing the whispered conversation, looked back through the trees and across the meadow to the pond. The aspens *were* a little far away, especially with coyote in the valley. But what could you do? You ate the trees closest to the pond first, and once they were gone, you had to risk going farther and farther into the woods or you wouldn't find anything to eat.

"Forget about how far away we are," growled the old beaver. "This is where the food is, so why don't you two stop wasting time and help me get it back to the pond."

"You mean this is where the food *was*," said one of the younger beavers, reluctantly moving toward the downed aspen. "Even if we take every one of these aspens down, we'll be lucky to make it through the winter."

"All the more reason to get to work now," snarled the older beaver.

"If you ask me, we ought to be working those birch trees on the other side of the pond—"

"But no one asked you," said the older beaver.

"All I'm saying is that we're going to have to move sooner or later, so what's the point of sticking around here until we run out of bark?"

"What's the point of wasting all this time talking when there's work to be done?" said the older beaver, tearing a small branch off with his teeth. "That's what I'd like to know."

"Ah, you old beavers are all alike," said the younger beaver. "You never heard a new idea you liked."

"A new idea, huh?" said the older beaver, looking over his shoulder. "Like the one your friend Three Paws had?"

Three Paws, in fact, had come to the same conclusion about the dwindling food supply earlier that summer, and had decided to set off on his own in search of a mate and another stream to dam up. A week later he had limped back to the pond, having gnawed through one of his paws to escape a trap.

"Yeah, that's what I thought," said the old beaver, when he got no response. "So why don't you two quit wasting time and stick to the plan, just like everybody else in the colony. We'll move when thecouncil says it's time to move."

"Just because Three Paws stepped into a trap doesn't mean

the rest of us should stay here until there's nothing left to eat," said the young beaver that had felled the tree, "or we end being eaten ourselves. The problem with the council is that they've gotten fat, happy, and lazy, *and* they've forgotten that there are other beavers in the forest, and that we're not going to be able to just stroll out of here and find a good stand of trees with a stream nearby whenever the mood hits them."

"And what is it with the poplar?" asked the other young beaver. "How about a little birch on the menu—"

"Or some willow bark?" continued the other young beaver.

"It's not about the kind of food, you young idiots," said the older beaver. "It's about the kind of food that's near the water."

The two young beavers looked at each other.

"Well," said one to the other, "maybe it's time we started coming at this from a different direction, and think about ways we can move the water, instead of moving to it."

The older beaver shook his head.

"Move the water? Next thing you'll be telling me is that we're going to start living in trees."

* * *

High above the valley a lone eagle soared through the evening sky, his wings spread wide. From his constantly shifting vantage point, he was able to track the movements of the animals on the ground, in the trees, and in the water. As he circled high above the valley, the black bear wandered out of the forest, and with a piercing shriek the eagle swooped down toward the meadow to take a closer look.

A turtle sunned herself on a rock at the edge of the pond, and as the eagle's shadow swept across her she instinctively yanked her head and legs back into her shell. Her hearing wasn't very good to start with, and now, with her head pulled back, she couldn't see anything either. Still, rather than face whatever was happening around her, she preferred to hide in her shell, hoping that when she stuck her head out again everything would be all right.

The Brush Fire

As the days grew shorter, and the leaves began to change color, men appeared in the valley again. They came over the eastern ridge of the valley late one afternoon, and they made so much noise doing it that every animal in the area knew they were coming. The men worked their way down the valley, and when they came to the meadow they set up camp near the aspen grove, thinking they would be sheltered from the wind.

They couldn't have been more wrong. Fanned by a relentless wind from the northeast, their fire flared up and threw sparks into the air all night long. The following morning, as the sky above the eastern horizon turned pink and blue, the men threw more wood on the fire and began to cook their breakfast. The ones who weren't cooking cleaned their rifles.

The deer hadn't stayed around long enough to find out which of the animals in the forest the men intended to shoot. While the buck never worried about grazing near coyote or bear, as soon as he caught the scent of the men his white tail pointed toward the sky, and his hooves pounded a drumbeat on the forest floor. The youngest deer were stunned. They had never known the buck to run away from something they couldn't even see. But the whole herd had taken off after him, so after a moment's hesitation the young ones took off, too, blindly following the other deer and figuring they'd ask questions later.

Later that morning, as the men broke camp, the eagle soared high above the valley, casually observing their movements. As he circled over the beaver pond the eagle spotted the black bear foraging farther up the valley. *Lucky for him,* thought the eagle, as the men headed west across the meadow. *He doesn't know how close he came to ending up as a rug in somebody's study.*

The eagle was right. The bear didn't have a clue. In fact, later that morning, when the wind shifted, the bear headed back down the stream again, skirted the pond, and went right to the abandoned campsite, drawn by the smell of garbage. The campfire was still burning. When he had finished picking through what he could find on the ground, the bear ambled over to the fire and pawed at a few of the branches, flipping one of them into the grass. The wind had picked up again by then, and as the bear watched the fire began to spread along the edge of the meadow. There hadn't been any rain for some time, so the flames ran ahead quickly, like leaves in the wind.

As soon as the eagle spotted smoke he circled down toward the meadow, his wings spread wide. Flying lower and lower, he saw the flames advancing across the grass, blackening the ground as they passed, and he let out a few piercing shrieks, alerting the animals that were still unaware of the danger. A red-tailed hawk appeared above him, also drawn by the smoke.

Fires were bad news for the animals of the forest, but not for the birds of prey. Just like the coyotes had, the flames would flush some of the smaller animals out into the open, and as they tried to escape one danger they risked falling victim to another.

It was already too late for many of them. The hawk, now gliding just above the blackened ground, snagged a dead rabbit in one of her talons and quickly lifted herself back into the air. The meadow was already strewn with the carcasses of mice, chipmunks, rabbits, and ground squirrels, all of whom could have outrun the flames, or hidden in their burrows, had they reacted in time. But none of them had ever seen a fire before, so they panicked, and with so much smoke in the air they didn't know which way to turn.

The gray squirrel had never seen a fire either, but she didn't plan to hang around long enough to learn anything about it. The screams of the smaller animals in the meadow and the acrid smell of the air told her everything she needed to know. And so, before the flames had gotten halfway across the meadow, she was running along branches, jumping from tree to tree, and putting as much distance as she could between herself and the brush fire.

Once the flames reached the far side of the meadow, they began to move into the forest. There the going was slower. The ground beneath the trees, untouched by sunlight, was covered with damp leaves, twigs, and pine needles, so the fire started to climb into the trees at the edge of the meadow.

The black bear, meanwhile, had made his way around the pond and had started to forage on the far side of the fire, completely unaware that it was now moving toward him. All he knew was that the heat was starting to force grubs and insects out into the open, and he licked them up greedily with his long tongue. Before long, though, the heat began to make even the bear a little uncomfortable, and cursing his bad luck he reluctantly moved off into the forest. By then the flames had already climbed into the lower branches of the trees at the edge of the meadow.

All at once there was a sizzling crack in the sky, followed by a drumroll of thunder, and then drenching rain. A low black cloud had burst right over the valley, and although the rain fell for only about fifteen or twenty minutes, by the time the sun appeared again the fire was all but out. Charred tree limbs still sizzled along the edge of the forest, and steam continued to curl off the meadow, but the brush fire was out.

* * *

The beavers didn't even know there had been a fire until they swam out of their lodges that evening. The first one out took a quick lap around the shore, his nose in the air. He quickly recognized the smell of burnt wood, although it wasn't too strong. Not much of a fire, he figured. The lodges hadn't been harmed, and neither had the branches they'd started piling up for the winter.

Continuing his rounds, the beaver saw something that made his eyes open wide—the aspen grove to the east of the meadow had caught fire, and the trees were still smoking. He smacked his tail against the water several times, and before long the other beavers poured out of their lodges, chattering among themselves. It didn't take long for them to see that there were only about twenty or thirty trees left standing. And with winter coming on, those trees were the last food within reach of the pond.

The fox cubs in the den slept right through the brush fire, too, piled one on top of the other in the deepest, darkest part of the den. The she-fox, however, had been awakened by the sounds of the fleeing animals, and by the smell of smoke, and as tired as she was, she crept up the tunnel and stuck her head out to see what was going on.

Unlike most of the animals in the valley, she'd lived

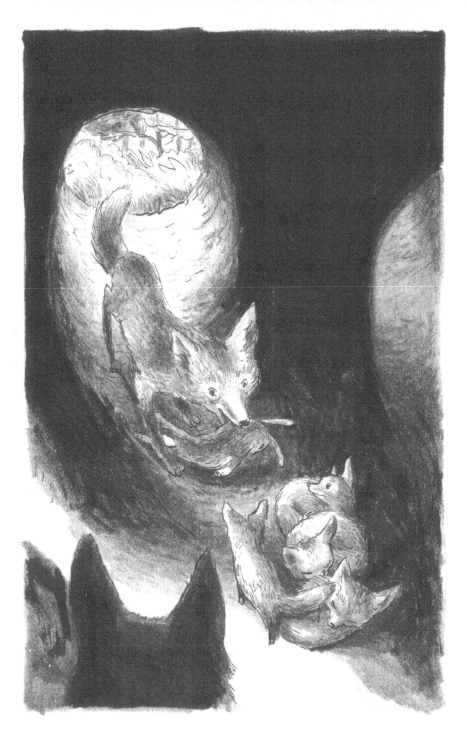

through several fires. All of them had been small, like the one burning in the meadow now, but far from bringing back bad memories, the fire made the she-fox remember how good the hunting had been after the fires had gone out. And as if to confirm those memories, a rabbit appeared out of the smoke and came hopping toward her. As quick as lightning she leapt out, grabbed the rabbit by the neck, and dragged it down into the tunnel. When she finally got the carcass into the den, she stopped to take a breath, and one of her cubs came over for a sniff.

"What's that smell?" asked the cub.

"That's the smell of fire…and smoke…and singed fur."

The cub backed up timidly.

"Is the fire going to get me, too?"

His mother nosed him back alongside his slumbering brothers and sisters.

"That's up to you. Fires are part of the forest, but that doesn't mean *you* have to get burned."

There was no point in waking the rest of the family. They'd have to be careful going in and out of the den now that the cover of the grass was gone, but she'd talk to them about that later. So she sent the one curious cub back to sleep, and before she curled up herself, she went to check the other entrance to the den. She wanted to be sure that they had plenty of air, and that the fire hadn't attracted any uninvited guests.

After the
Brush Fire

Although the blackened trees at the edge of the meadow bore silent witness to the destructive power of fire, the sudden rainstorm had kept the flames from spreading across the valley, which in itself was but one small part of the great forest that surrounded it. As a result, almost as soon as the smoke cleared, the animals that hadn't been hurt started to return to the meadow, anxious to see what, if anything, was left of their homes.

Used to moving through the forest at high speed, the gray squirrel was one of the first to return. She leapt from branch to branch, high above the ground, until she found herself in familiar territory.

It wasn't that bad. Looked like she'd lost only one nest. As she assessed the situation, a furious *rat-a-tat-tatting* came from above. Startled, she looked up to see the woodpecker chipping a hole into the trunk halfway up the tree.

"Hey, woodpecker. Give it a rest, would you? It's bad enough having to look at what this brush fire did to the meadow without listening to that racket."

The woodpecker thought it over for a moment, then

scooted down the trunk until he was at the same level as the squirrel.

"Lost everything, eh?"

Turning her head, the gray squirrel clucked at the woodpecker.

"You must be confusing me with the red squirrel," she said. "I'm not stupid enough to put all my acorns in one tree."

And with that, she ran off toward the end of the branch, threw herself into the air, and disappeared into the next tree, the leaves rustling behind her.

Looking around, the woodpecker saw other squirrels moving through the trees, too, and a hawk circling just above them. In the middle of the scorched meadow a turkey vulture fed on a carcass. As the woodpecker watched it tear strips of meat from the limp ball of fur in its talon, a commotion started up on the edge of the meadow. The fat red squirrel was on the ground, chattering away and pointing to the charred remains of the massive oak he had called home.

"What am I going to do now?" he moaned. "I've got nothing to eat, and nowhere to live."

Suddenly the squirrel went silent, and then vanished on the far side of another tree. A moment later the black bear appeared. He sniffed at the charred bark of the oak tree for a moment, then raised his head and looked up at the woodpecker.

"Afternoon, bear."

The bear gave him a curt nod.

"Finding plenty to eat down there?" asked the woodpecker.

The black bear nodded, stuck his nose into a pile of sodden leaves, and then pinned a mouse to the ground with one enormous paw as it tried to escape.

"The hardest part is deciding what to eat first," he said, taking the mouse in his teeth and gulping it down.

"Any sign of those hunters?"

The bear raked the leaves with his claws, hoping he'd find more than one mouse.

"What hunters?"

* * *

Later that same afternoon, the fox's snout slowly appeared out of the mouth of one of the main tunnels leading to her den. A charred tree had fallen across the back entrance, and although air still circulated through the burrow, getting the cubs out safely wouldn't be easy. With her ears raised, the she-fox cautiously sniffed the air, and then pushed her head above ground, peering right and left. Nearby, she saw a turkey vulture feeding on a rabbit carcass, and seeing the hawks circling above the meadow, she decided to stay put until nightfall.

As she crept back down the tunnel, she decided she'd better get to work digging a new exit as soon as it got dark. That way, she and her cubs wouldn't run the risk of being trapped by some burrowing predator. Curling up next to her cubs, she toyed with the idea of adding a third exit, too. One entrance now let out in the middle of a burned-out meadow, and the other beneath a fallen tree at the meadow's edge. The smart

thing would be to dig another tunnel. Maybe one that came out in the forest.

The beavers didn't know the extent of the fire until later that afternoon, because the pond that kept their predators at bay also kept their homes and their food from burning. As soon as they saw what had happened to the stand of aspens, though, they knew the colony was in trouble. Now they were going to have to travel even farther to find food, and they were going to have to take even bigger risks doing it. And they weren't the only beavers in the valley, either, which meant they'd have to move quickly.

"All right, you beavers," said one of the older members of the colony, giving the water a sharp slap with his tail. "Quiet down and listen up. We've only got a couple months before the pond ices over, so we've got to get to work. I want to see every one of those aspens cut down, chewed to pieces, and dragged into the pond as soon as possible."

One of the younger beavers spoke up.

"Is your nose clogged, or did you lose your sense of smell?"

The old beaver snarled and started toward him.

"Don't be a tough guy, old-timer," said the young beaver, rising up on his hind legs.

The older beaver kept coming, and everyone turned to watch them face off.

"Have it your way," said the young beaver, "but if you had any sense you'd put your nose in the air, and save me the trouble of kicking your old, silver-haired butt."

The old beaver stopped short, and one by one he and the rest of the beavers in the colony began to sniff the air, moving their heads from side to side.

"That's right," said the young beaver. "Our old friends the coyotes are back in the valley. So if you listen to grandpa here, and try to get to those aspens tonight, you're going to wind up as somebody's late-night snack."

A number of the beavers began talking all at once. Others slipped back into the water, just in case the coyotes were closer than they thought.

* * *

Later that night, after things had calmed down, several of the beavers snuck off to the far side of the pond. The young beaver that had spoken up that afternoon sat on his hind-quarters and called for quiet.

"Listen up," he said, putting his forepaws in the air. "Me and a couple of the other beavers are thinking about striking out on our own. You know, looking for a place where we don't have to risk not finding enough food to last through the winter."

"And where're we gonna find a place like that?"

"On the far side of that ridge," said the young beaver, pointing to the west. "All the deer that come through here say that valley's full of birch and aspen—"

"So what? There's no water there."

"Not now, there isn't," he said, nodding his head in agreement. "But a couple of us have been talking it over, and we figure we could build a dam farther up the valley. You know, in front of one of the smaller streams. And if we build it high enough, we should be able to steer the water right over the ridge."

"Build a dam farther up the valley?" snorted one of the older beavers. "Steer water over the ridge? Have you and your friends been chewing stinkweed again? No beaver has ever done anything like that. Are you crazy? You think you can just waddle up the valley, throw a dam up in a couple of weeks, and change the course of a stream?"

"No, I think it'll take about a month," he said, looking around at the beavers there, "which means there'll have to be at least nine or ten of us."

"It wouldn't matter if there were twenty of you. The days are already getting shorter. You'd be risking your lives for nothing."

The young beaver smoothed his whiskers back.

"I'll take that risk. And you want to know why? Because I think staying here is an even bigger risk. There isn't much food left, not after the brush fire, and if anything else goes wrong—"

"What else could go wrong?"

"Plenty. And if it does, everyone who stays here is going to starve."

The buck led the deer back into the valley about a week

later. When the herd came to the blackened meadow and the charred trees, they simply pushed on until they found another opening in the forest, farther to the west, carpeted with grass and surrounded by bushes. The woodpecker found them there later that afternoon, and came to rest on a tree limb just in front of the buck.

"Glad to see you and the herd weren't caught in the fire."

The buck stopped chewing his cud.

"We were running from the hunters, not the fire."

"They were headed your way when the fire broke out, weren't they?"

The buck nodded, his antlers bobbing.

"Once I picked up their scent, though, I took the herd south, and then we circled back around to the other side of the valley."

"So no one got caught in the fire."

The buck shook his head.

"I'm glad to hear it," said the woodpecker. "But with all due respect, just because you didn't get burned this time doesn't mean you're fireproof."

* * *

The brush fire wasn't a disaster for all the animals in the forest—for some, it was a stroke of luck. The leafless trees and the blackened ground made hunting a lot easier, not that there had been any need to hunt right away, since the meadow was littered with dead animals. In fact, even before the ground had stopped smoking the boldest of the scavengers had landed and started to feed. The air was alive with insects, too, and as the vultures feasted on rabbits, mice, and chipmunks, the songbirds flew back and forth across the meadow, eating their fill.

For the animals who survived, it seemed like the valley was even more dangerous *after* the brush fire. Even if their nests hadn't been destroyed, or their seeds and nuts hadn't gone up in smoke, the changed landscape and the mob of predators greatly increased the number of risks. But the feast didn't last long. Within a week the valley floor was nearly empty. Prey that was usually taken over time, allowing the animal population to rebuild, was wiped out in the space of a few days, so in the end the predators had little choice but to move on, too.

Once that happened, the animals just beyond the path of the brush fire quickly returned to their old ways of life. Most had never seen a brush fire before, and would never see one again, so they quickly forgot about it. Sure, it had been frightening, just like thunderstorms were frightening. But since none of them had ever been *struck* by lightning, none of them worried about it.

Regeneration

The forest's natural cycle of growth, destruction, and regeneration depends as much on fire as it does on rain. And soon after the brush fire was out, that cycle began again. The fire destroyed a meadow full of grass already gone to seed, but only a few weeks later, green shoots of grass began to push their way up out of the blackened ground. The destruction of some of the older, more mature trees along the edge of the forest allowed the smaller trees beneath them to bask in the sunlight. Even the scorched bushes under the beaver dam, which the flames had only partially consumed, quickly began to put out fresh young leaves. So although the brush fire took the lives of some animals, and destroyed the homes of others, it also performed a valuable service—it cleaned out that part of the valley, disturbed the established order, and gave new life a chance.

Of course, most of the animals on the ground didn't see it that way. They lived such short lives that they came across fires only once, or twice at the most, and when they did they thought about only one thing—running away before they got burned. None of them ever said to themselves afterward: *that's more like it—a brush fire is just what this part of the forest needed.* Instead, they feared fire. It was something they couldn't control. It was something that took their homes. That took the food they ate. And sometimes it even took their lives. But since it was so rare, once it had come and gone, it was easy to forget all about it, especially if it didn't force any changes in the way they lived.

The gray squirrel, for instance, paid almost no attention to the new growth in the meadow; she was building another nest to replace the one she'd lost to the brush fire. And when she finally ventured out into the meadow again, foraging for food, she didn't pay any attention to the grass pushing its way up through the ashes of the brush fire. There had always been grass in the meadow, and before long there would be grass again. She didn't see why everybody made such a big fuss about fires. As long as you had food stored in more than one place you'd never go hungry.

As she darted off, looking for fallen nuts, the buck appeared at the edge of the meadow. The herd waited in the shadows behind him. Once he was satisfied that it was safe, he led the other deer out into the meadow, and they began to feed on the fresh green grass.

* * *

Farther up the valley, the black bear was on the prowl. He hadn't given the brush fire a second thought. Just like always, he was thinking about his next meal. There was still a funny sort of smell in the air, he had to admit, but he was more interested in the rotting log at his feet. Tearing it open with his claws, he found what he'd been looking for, and as the bugs rushed for cover he scooped them up with his long tongue.

Near the edge of the pond, the turtle clambered out of the water and onto a partially submerged log. The smell of charred wood hung heavily in the air, and with a slow turn of her head she took in all the changes in the landscape.

Always a little frightening coming out of your shell, she thought. *You never know what you're going to find. Still, I like it better in the dark water at the bottom of the pond than out here in the open. You don't have to worry about things you can't see.*

* * *

The she-fox had returned to her old way of life, too, but she hadn't forgotten the brush fire, and was well aware of the way it had altered the landscape in that part of the forest.

"How come we're going out this way?" one of her cubs asked, following her up the tunnel that led to the back entrance.

"Because with the dead tree there we'll be harder to see."

"But why can't we just go out the way we used to?"

"Because everything else is always changing," she said, watching her cubs troop out, "and we have to change, too."

* * *

The beavers that stayed behind had started to feel a little better about their chances of making it through the winter.

They'd cut down every last aspen within reach of the pond, and what they hadn't eaten immediately they'd dragged into the water, where they'd be able to get to it once the pond froze over. Plus, there weren't as many of them as there used to be.

The beavers that had left the colony were miles away, hard at work at the top of the valley. They were just putting the finishing touches on the dam that would raise the level of the water in one of the smaller streams until it spilled over the ridge. Their young leader clambered up onto the mud and sticks, and surveyed the scene. Although the brush fire hadn't reached that part of the valley, the memory of the blackened aspens was still fresh in his mind, and the thought of it energized him whenever he wondered whether leaving the colony had been a mistake.

Just another day or two and we'll be done here, he thought, *and then the real work starts. Once we've got the water flowing into the valley to the west, we've got to get another dam in place, just below those aspens. And then we've got to get to work on a lodge.* He looked to the north, across the forest, where the leaves were already starting to change color.

The Forest Fire

As the days grew shorter and the nights grew colder, the animals in the valley prepared themselves for winter. Most of them had forgotten all about the brush fire, and had gone back to doing things exactly the way they had always done them, almost as if the meadow had never caught fire—and maybe even more importantly, as if it would never catch fire again. This was especially true of the animals that hadn't been hurt, or hadn't lost anything in the brush fire. They'd been through one fire, and nothing much had happened—at least not to them—so what was the point in worrying about another?

Indian summer had settled over the forest later than usual that fall. The sun had shone brightly every day, and no rain had fallen, so the leaves and twigs and brush on the forest floor were as dry as old bones. The grass in the meadow had turned brown, too, and the streams had slowed to a trickle. Worst of all, the men in the forest had done such a good job of keeping smaller fires under control that years and years had gone by without a true forest fire. The valley, in other words, was populated with animals that did little or nothing to manage the risk of fire, just as that risk was growing.

Finally, one morning, when the air was warmer than usual and rain clouds formed a dark ceiling over the valley, the animals were startled by a sudden, crackling explosion. A deep, rumbling thunder followed the lightning strike, and by the time the thunder faded away, a stand of old, dead pine trees was in flames.

Within minutes, burning branches began to fall to the forest floor, and not long after that, the trees themselves shuddered and fell into the arms of the trees closest to them. Before long those trees were also in flames. The brush on the ground had caught fire, too, and pushed along by a steady northeasterly wind, the flames started to move down the valley. Small at first, the fire spread quickly, feeding on the dry undergrowth as it moved from one tree to another. The smoke, driven ahead by the wind, alerted every animal in the valley that the forest was on fire. Still, the smoke was no thicker than it had been with the brush fire, at least not at first, so the animals downwind weren't too worried. As the first crucial minutes passed, however, and with them the opportunity to react while there was still time, many of those animals missed their one chance to escape. Within an hour of the time the lightning struck, the peaceful valley had become an inferno. The flames now rose high above the trees, advancing through the forest like a tidal wave of fire.

The gray squirrel, a mile or so from the flames, didn't wait around to find out what had happened. As soon as the first whiff of smoke reached her, she began to run. After all, running had always saved her before—even from fire. Yes, she was probably going to lose more seeds and nuts, but she had nests spread throughout that part the valley, and the fire wouldn't get to all of them. Besides, a light drizzle had started to fall, so this fire would probably end the same way the last one had.

But it didn't, not this time, and the gray squirrel had to keep on running. She ran and she ran and she ran, and before she knew it, she was in a part of the forest she'd never seen before. But there was no time to stop and think, because the fire kept coming.

As the rising wind pushed the fire to the south, the flames burned hotter and hotter, spreading rapidly across the valley and continuing their relentless march through the forest. This time, when the flames reached the meadow they seemed to leap across the new grass, and none of the animals on the ground escaped, their screams swallowed up by the howling blaze.

The buck caught the scent of smoke soon after the lightning bolt struck the dead trees. He let the herd continue to feed even as the fire grew, and started to make its way down the valley. In fact, long after all the birds had taken wing, and the turtles had plopped into the water, and the burrowing animals had scurried down into their dens, the deer continued to feed, the grass still wet with the morning's dew. Just like the gray squirrel, the buck believed he could outrun anything, and because he was the fastest animal in the forest, he was in no rush.

The roar of the advancing flames, though, and the unnatural heat, started to make him think that this fire was different from any he'd seen before. Even though the fire itself was still hundreds of yards away, the herd was slowly forced back by the smoke and the heat. Still, the buck retreated only as far as he had to, and then stopped to graze again. And although a few of the younger deer wondered about the wisdom of staying so close to the crackling, sizzling flames, the rest waited for a sign from their leader, just like they always did.

As the buck continued to feed, almost daring the fire to come nearer, another lightning bolt struck to the south. Before long a stand of trees below the field was in flames, too, and now there was no longer a clear path of escape. The fire continued to send sparks high into the air, and pushed forward by the wind, they touched off smaller fires on all sides of the valley. The heat was now so intense that the trees closest to the blaze began to explode into flames, and the buck, never having seen anything like this before, experienced his first moment of panic. By then the herd was surrounded by fire. Blinded by the smoke, and terrified by the heat, the buck ran from one part of the field to another, unable to find a way out. Finally, as the fire closed in on all sides, he ran blindly into the smoke—and directly into the hottest part of the inferno. Every deer in the herd followed him, and all of them suffered a horrible, agonizing death.

* * *

As the fire grew, it continued to change direction without warning, and the black bear, halfway up a beech tree, was caught by surprise. He'd seen the smoke, of course, and had heard the screams of the animals in the distance, but he hadn't paid much attention. The only thing he cared about was making sure he got to every nut on this tree.

And so, he continued to eat, cracking one nut after another in his powerful jaws. Suddenly the sky went dark, and he heard the trunks of pine trees exploding in the distance. *Just my luck*, he thought, shaking his head in annoyance. *You don't find a tree like this every day, especially so late in the season, and if that fire gets any closer I'm going to have to climb down before I'm done.* He cracked another couple of nuts, but as the sound of fire grew louder he reluctantly started backing down the tree.

Things didn't look so bad on the ground. The fire didn't seem as close as it had when he was up the tree, and the bear wondered if he had time for a few more nuts. The fire kept getting louder and louder, though, and that puzzled the bear. It almost sounded like the fire was gasping for breath, like a winded animal. In fact, the fire seemed to be pulling the air right toward it, and although the bear put his nose in the air he couldn't decide which way he ought to go to avoid the flames. Finally, he turned to the south, consoling himself with the thought of all the carcasses he'd feast on once the fire had passed.

As he loped along, though, thinking of roasted rabbits and mice, the air suddenly got hotter. He skidded to a stop, not sure what to do, and as he stood there, panting, the fire showed itself through the smoke. For the first time he saw the wall of flames, and realized it was coming right for him.

Terrified, he wheeled and galloped off in the other direction. But it seemed like the faster he ran, the faster the fire came after him, driven by the gusting wind. He could feel the

heat behind him, and, clambering up the western ridge, he wondered for the first time in his life whether he had taken a risk he shouldn't have—a risk he could easily have avoided.

He should have taken off as soon as he smelled the smoke. All it would have cost him was a handful of beechnuts. But there was no time to think about that now. If he could just get to the top of the ridge before the fire did, he might get away. So, gathering all the strength he had left, he broke free of the forest, clawed his way to the top of the ridge, and clambered up onto a dirt road. Exhausted, and blinded by the smoke, he paused to catch his breath.

Didn't think I was going to make it there for a minute. Who knew a fire could get that big, or move that fast? Never seen anything like it.

As he stood there, turning first one way and then another, he heard the whine of something going past his head, followed by a deafening blast. Confused by the noise, and not sure which way to turn, he watched as a gust of wind opened a hole in the smoke, and for the first time he could see down the road. A man stood facing him. The man had a rifle in his hands, and raising it to his shoulder, he pointed it at the bear and fired.

The bear never heard the shot.

* * *

Far below the ground, safe in their den, the she-fox and her cubs shuddered as they listened to the fire, and to the cries of its victims. She had lived through a number of fires, but she knew right away that this was something different. For one thing, it didn't crackle and pop like a brush fire—it howled like the wind. The cries of the animals were different, too. They were coming from everywhere. This fire wasn't going to burn out quickly, not that she had any thoughts of leaving the den. The whole valley was probably in flames, and the smoke would be so thick you wouldn't be able to see more than a few feet in front of you. The best thing to do was to stay put.

Then, she heard a sound she'd never heard before. It was a sort of gurgling sound, and it was coming right toward them. It sounded almost like water. Like water running along a streambed. And sure enough, as she got up to investigate, cold water surged into the den.

From her hiding place far beneath the surface of the meadow, she could not know that an enormous pine tree had fallen across the beaver dam, and that after it burned there for a while the dam had finally collapsed.

At first the water from the pond had surged out across the meadow, extinguishing the flames in front of it. Then it began to flood into the tunnels and burrows beneath the ground. With only seconds to think, and three escape routes to choose from, she quickly decided to lead her cubs into the one she'd dug after the brush fire—the only one that didn't come out in the meadow.

There was no time to lose. They could all hear the water

splashing behind them as they made their way up the dark tunnel. Finally, the she-fox saw a flickering orange light ahead of her. So the woods were on fire, too. But the water had almost reached them by then, so she and her cubs had only two choices—either drown, or risk being burned alive.

Barking for her cubs to follow her, she leapt out into the blast furnace. Nothing looked like it had before, but getting her bearings as best she could, she raced off to where she thought the next burrow should be. Luck was with her, though, and when she got to the entrance, she stopped and watched the cubs go down the tunnel in front of her, then dove in after them. When she had crawled all the way down into the dark den, she moved from one cub to another, making sure they were all right. One hadn't made it. Her heart sank, and for a moment she thought about going back out. But she knew she couldn't.

The cubs that *had* survived needed her. Their paws were burned and their fur was scorched. But they were alive. And while they were all trapped for the time being, at least they'd thought to leave a little food in the burrow. And so, exhausted by their ordeal, the she-fox and her cubs settled down to wait until the fire had passed, hoping that the cubs' father had survived, too.

But the she-fox couldn't sleep. She was still wondering about her mate, and thinking about the cub that didn't make it. She knew that cubs didn't always survive to have cubs of their own. It was the way of the forest. But she felt she'd let her family down. She'd seen the dry leaves piling up. She'd known there hadn't been any rain for weeks. And she'd known there

hadn't been a fire in the forest, a fire like the one howling above them, for many, many years. So while the fire was inevitable, she had never even considered what she was going to do when the inevitable finally happened.

* * *

The collapse of the dam had caught the beavers by surprise, too. They had stayed in their lodges at first, and by the time they realized what was happening the pond was already half empty. By then, the fire was so loud that there was no way to communicate; everyone had to look out for himself. The trees that ringed the pond were all on fire, and one by one they began to fall, sometimes toward the burning forest, and sometimes toward the terrified beavers.

Although she had dug her way into the mud as far as she could go, not even the turtle could pretend that nothing was going on. As one tree after another crashed to the ground the mud shook like she'd never felt it shake before, and as the water poured out of the pond she could sense the beavers' frantic movements above her.

* * *

Thousands of men poured into the forest, and they did everything they could to contain the fire—including starting their own fires, over which they quickly lost control. But the wall of flames continued its ruthless advance. Only when clouds filled the sky again, and a heavy rain began to fall, did the fire finally go out.

A day later, the eagle reappeared above the valley.

After the Forest Fire

Soaring high above the meadow, the eagle surveyed the gray, lifeless landscape stretching to the south. He had been many miles away when the fire broke out, and by the time he was aware of what was happening, the heat was so intense and the smoke so thick that he had been unable to go anywhere near it. Now, with the flames extinguished, the terrain had changed so completely that he had trouble finding his way back to the valley. Stripped of their leaves and branches, the blackened trees now stood shoulder to shoulder like mourners at a funeral. A thick layer of soot and ash covered the meadow.

Only a week earlier, the forest had been a shifting green ocean of sound and movement, of leaves and branches swaying in the wind, of animals moving along the ground, leaping through the trees and darting swiftly through the air. Now, an eerie silence reigned.

Something moved near the charred remains of the beaver dam, and circling lower, the eagle saw a raccoon feeding on a turtle.

* * *

The gray squirrel was far to the west. She had run so far, in fact, that she would never have been able to find her way back, even if there had been anything to come back to. But her relief at having escaped death disappeared almost as soon as she stopped panting for air. There were now thousands of squirrels in that part of the forest. The others had outrun the fire, just like the gray squirrel had, but now they all found themselves in unfamiliar territory. And none of them had nests or food. Worse still, most of the trees and the bushes had already been picked clean of seeds and nuts.

A few weeks after the fire, the first snow fell, making it even harder for the gray squirrel to sniff out anything to eat on the ground. And although she continued to forage, she was beginning to understand that she had survived the fire, but wouldn't live to see the spring.

The fox and her cubs, observing the mass migration to the west, decided instead to strike out for the north. Two nights later, they climbed a mountain range and looked down on a northern-facing valley, a mirror image of the one they'd just left. Before the sun rose the following day, the fox's mate had found an abandoned burrow, and the two of them settled the cubs into it before they went out to hunt. Winter wasn't far off, but there was still game in the valley, and not too much competition, it seemed. By the end of the winter they would be all fur and bones, but if they were lucky, they and the cubs would survive.

* * *

When the rain finally put out the last hissing embers, the beavers emerged from the shallow, sooty pools of water in which they'd hidden to find their world transformed. Their elaborate system of defense had been destroyed, there was nothing left to eat in the valley, and winter was on its way.

They huddled together, talking among themselves, but everyone knew what they had to do. So that night they headed up the stream, which was now choked with ashes, charred branches, and dead fish. But they weren't the only animals left in the valley. A pack of coyotes had crossed the eastern ridge a few hours earlier, and in the bright moonlight the beavers were easy pickings. Only five of them escaped.

When they reached the top of the western ridge, and looked down into the next valley, they were stunned to see that the trees in the forest still had their leaves. Even more startling was the sight of a small pond, its surface glittering in the moonlight. As they straggled down toward it they could see beavers crisscrossing its waters with branches in their mouths, some of them strengthening the dam, others enlarging the lodge at its center. The survivors made their way down the slope and quickly realized that these were the beavers that had abandoned the colony only a few months earlier, right after the brush fire. Who knew if they'd even take them in, after all the fighting that had gone on?

They needn't have worried. Their old pond mates welcomed them with open paws, surprised that any of them had survived the forest fire. But there would be time to catch up later. The forest fire had greatly increased the risks in the area—mostly in the form of roving coyotes—so even though the colony had added a few new members, they still had their work cut out for them.

Applying the
Lessons
of the Story

Whether you realize it or not, you now know a lot more about risk management than you did when you opened this book. But before we begin teasing lessons out of this tale, I'd like you to look over the following list, and then, with as much honesty as your pride will allow, choose the animal whose approach to risk management most closely resembles your own. (You might, of course, see yourself in more than one animal, so feel free to make a list.)

Red Squirrel: you keep all your acorns in one tree.
Rabbit: you change your approach to risk over and over again.
Black Bear: you're oblivious to risk.
Gray Squirrel: you store your acorns in many different places.
Deer: you blindly follow the herd (which blindly follows a single buck).
Red Fox: you're *aware* of the risks around you, and you have a process in place to manage them; in some cases, you even benefit from them.
Beaver: you're one of two types. The first believes in sticking to plans and following orders from upstairs. The second

believes in taking risks, especially after having arrived at the conclusion that doing things the way they've always been done amounts to the biggest risk of all.

Turtle: you know that you're surrounded by risks, but rather than face them, you prefer to stay in your shell and hope for the best.

Now that you've made your pick, think back to what happened to *your* animal during the story's two pivotal events—the brush fire and the forest fire. The brush fire was the animals' first test as risk managers, and while it revealed the strengths of some, it also *concealed* the weaknesses of others. In other words, some of the animals' approaches were *deceptively* effective, succeeding only by chance, or because they weren't put to a real test. The gray squirrel's hoards of seeds and nuts, for example, scattered throughout the valley as they were, kept her from suffering serious losses as a result of the brush fire. But the same approach failed completely in the systemic disaster of the forest fire.

This was true of many of the animals that survived the brush fire—they *mistakenly* believed they were capable of surviving a truly catastrophic fire, too. What's more, few of them took the time to consider what they'd do *after* a big fire, when they would face another set of risks—risks for which they were completely unprepared, because they'd never even considered them. Nor did they ever consider that the damage done by a fire isn't limited to the area of the burn. Those animals that escape death still lose their food and their homes, and are driven into the territories of other animals—animals with whom they'll have to compete for scarce resources. In this way, the animal populations of the areas surrounding the fire will become victims of the fire, too, even though the flames never actually reached them.

Keeping those things in mind, let's look at the animals one by one, review the way things turned out for them, and then think about what each of them might have done differently—and what you might do differently, too, if you continue to approach risk the way they did.

The Red Squirrel did a lot of things right. He worked hard, and he saved. But he made one critical mistake—he kept all his acorns in one tree. And not only that, he stored them in the tree he *lived* in. As a result, a simple brush fire wiped out both his home and his savings. This sort of risk concentration, surprisingly enough, is common even among the well-educated and the well-off. Think, for instance, of the many companies that have collapsed over the past twenty years, where the workforce lost not only their jobs, but their retirement savings, too, because their 401(k) accounts contained nothing but company stock.

The Lesson: If you're a Red Squirrel, you should think about dividing your assets between different institutions (i.e., banks, credit unions, and investment firms) and across different asset classes (i.e., bonds, stocks, real estate, commodities, and cash). Yes, this requires some work, and may even require some help, but it's better to do the work while you can—that is, while you still have some assets to invest. In other words, don't put it off any longer, because while the inevitable may take its time coming, when it does come, it comes quickly.

The Rabbit was fast on his feet, and had great hearing. He could also change his diet as the seasons changed. But he lacked one crucial personality trait: consistency. And by changing his approach—first staying on the move, then blending into the background—he ended up having no real approach at all. So, *even though the flames didn't kill him*, the rabbit became one of the brush fire's first victims. Panicked by the heat and the smoke, the rabbit started running in circles, and the fox, from the safety of her burrow, just had to wait until he came within reach.

The Lesson: If you're a Rabbit, you need to decide on a single, unified approach to risk management. If you can't do this on your own, get some good advice. That advice might come from a friend or colleague, or it might come from a professional advisor—but keep in mind that free advice is rarely worth more than you pay for it.

Start by asking yourself where you are today. Next, ask yourself where you want to be, and when you want to be there. And then come up with a simple process to manage the risks you'll encounter along the way—and to identify the sort of risks you may need to take to reach your goals. While that process won't guarantee success, you'll be in far better shape when disaster strikes, because you'll *already* have thought through what might happen, and how you'll react to it if it does. In other words, you can't avoid risk, but you can choose the risks you'll take.

The Black Bear was completely oblivious to danger. As a result, he never looked for the safest path; he just followed his nose toward his next meal. He never made plans, never considered the terrain, and never thought about what might happen if he headed north instead of south. And who could blame him? Given his size, his strength, his claws, and his teeth—to say nothing of his bone-rattling roar—what could possibly harm him?

But as it turned out, of course, there were animals in the forest able and willing to challenge the bear—as long as they had rifles in their hands. And even if there hadn't been hunters in the forest, not even bears are fireproof. So, while the hunters didn't succeed in tracking the bear down, they were ready to strike when the forest fire put him in front of them. As a result, the bear, just like the red squirrel and the rabbit, became a secondary casualty of the fire.

The Lesson: If you're a Black Bear, it's time you faced the facts. No matter how much money you have, or how powerful you believe yourself to be, you too are surrounded by risks. And the front pages of the newspapers are full of stories of people like you, who thought they were safe from any disaster—right up until the moment they lost everything. Even bears have to recognize risk, and learn to manage it, because the biggest risks are the ones we fail to consider.

The Gray Squirrel had a well-thought-out strategy. To begin with, she was industrious. She ate less than she gathered, and she diversified the *location* of her holdings—but only in her neck of the woods. That strategy worked well during the brush fire, but failed completely when the entire forest caught fire. And with no "foreign" holdings, once she had been driven from her habitat, she had no contingency plan to get her through the winter months in an unfamiliar place, where the local squirrel population had already harvested all the food.

The Lesson: If you're a Gray Squirrel, you, unlike the red squirrel, diversified your holdings, and as a result the brush fire didn't cause you much trouble. But the forest fire taught you that diversification rarely works *within a disaster zone*. In a forest fire, almost all the trees burn—and even if some of yours don't, you still might end up cut off from your remaining assets. So you want to be sure you always have enough cash *on hand* to stay in the game after the fire's out.

The Deer had survived for years because of their natural speed, and the watchful eye of the buck. But while their risk management strategy kept them out of range of the hunters' rifles, it failed entirely when the whole forest caught fire. And it failed because the herd put all its trust in one buck—a buck who had never faced a forest fire before, and therefore didn't know how to react. His failure to recognize the risk—before it was too late—led not only to his death, but to the deaths of all the deer that had followed him so blindly.

The Lesson: If you're a Deer, you've got a lot of company. How many times have you followed the crowd, selling when the market is near the bottom, and buying only after the bubble is inflated? Make your own decisions, or have them made for you, with your guidance—but don't follow the herd. They'll lead you into green pastures one day, and into an inferno the next.

The Red Fox, as you'll have figured out by now, is a model risk manager. She never stopped thinking about the risks she faced, and made plans long before she needed them. So, even though the brush fire didn't harm her, her mate, or her cubs, it made her think. What if the next disaster was different in some way? Would two escape routes be enough, especially if they both led to the meadow?

In addition to being prepared, she was always aware of the *opportunities* certain threats might offer her. And because she was always looking for an advantage, instead of running for cover, she learned to adapt her behavior to the conditions she found. The fox, in short, took advantage of risks that most forest dwellers avoided.

So, when the forest fire caused a flood—an almost unforeseeable event—she had already thought far enough ahead to dig a new exit. And that exit wasn't far from another burrow, and she hadn't forgotten to leave a little food in it. Finally, when it was clear that the valley was no longer habitable, she was mentally prepared to move her family to a new location, regardless of the season, and start again.

The Lesson: Constantly reassess the risks around you. But in addition to protecting yourself from those risks, remember to keep an eye out for *opportunities* that might accompany them. If you were looking to buy a house, for instance, you might rent until the market turns in your favor—i.e., when others, who bought when prices were high, will be eager to sell for whatever they can get. And no matter how carefully you've made your plans, be sure to consider exit strategies, too. All good risk managers know when it's time to cut their losses, and have thought ahead to how they'll get out if they need to.

The Beaver, finally, managed risk by altering the environment itself. They didn't look for advantages, they *created* them, and their ponds, lodges, and food stores represented the most comprehensive approach to risk management in the forest. That said, as with any organization, the beaver colony was dependent on the supply of goods, and had to compete with other colonies in the valley. And like all organizations, theirs was always at risk of failing to *adapt* to changing conditions.

In fact, in our story the beavers were divided between those that believed they were safe where they were, and those that believed the time had come to move—to take a risk. Sound familiar? As I said, the ways of the forest aren't really very different from our own. The more conservative beavers resisted change, and wanted nothing to do with risks that could be avoided—or at least put off. The beavers that looked ahead, instead, thought that staying put was a bigger risk than trying something new.

But they didn't just *choose* the risk they'd take, they chose a new way of *managing* that risk. For as long as anyone could remember, beavers had always looked for water first, and then for the nearest food. The beavers that moved out of the valley began by finding food, and then figured out how to bring water to it.

And as it turned out, they were the only animals in the valley that escaped harm. Yes, the wind might have changed, and the fire might have crossed the western ridge. But it didn't.

In other words, in this story, just like in life, luck often favors those who take risks.

The Lesson: Be proactive, not reactive. Understand that the natural tendency to continue doing things the same way is one of the biggest risks out there, because when changes come, they tend to come all at once. So once again, while you can't avoid risk, you can choose the risks you'll take.

The Turtle. Turtles don't try to manage risk; they do everything they can to ignore it. And when they can't ignore it, they try to hide from it.

The Lesson: Turtles can't run, and they can't hide either. At least not for long. Risks surround us all, and one day, those who willfully ignore such risks will almost certainly become their victims. What's worse, if you're a turtle you'll never really get a good night's sleep, because you can't *manage* risks you won't face.

* * *

The Rat Snake, the Eagle, and the Woodpecker: You've probably noticed that a few of the animals in this story didn't make the list at the beginning of this section. They form a group of their own, and I'm sure a lot of you know animals just like them.

The Rat Snake is an example of the fast-talking salesperson who says he knows what's best for you, but is really concerned with what's best for *him*. So when the snake offered to keep an eye on the red squirrel's acorns, he was really just looking for a chance to grab a few when the squirrel wasn't paying attention.

The Eagle was supposed to remain above it all. He was supposed to keep an eye on everything going on below. But he was nowhere to be found when the forest fire broke out, and by the time he returned to the valley, the damage was done.

The Woodpecker, instead, flew through the forest offering simple, practical advice, most of which he learned by observing how the other animals managed risk. In addition, he encouraged every animal to adopt a simple approach to risk management, and to stick to it. By doing that, he said, they'd be far more likely to survive the next fire—to say nothing of sleeping better at night.

The Lesson: If you don't feel comfortable managing risk yourself, be extremely careful when choosing someone to manage it for you.

Conclusion

Life without risk is a contradiction in terms. But it doesn't follow that we can't *choose* the risks we'll take in life. Strangely enough, though, the hardest part for most people seems to be getting started, so I wrote this story hoping to get you thinking about risk management before you even realized you were doing it. Once you begin to consider the risks around you, and take the time to learn just a few basic principles of risk management, the rest begins to fall into place. Then, knowing what kind of a risk animal you really are, all you need to do is ask yourself the following three questions: what do you want, when do you want it, and what will you risk to get it? If you can do that, you're on your way.

But keep in mind that risk management isn't a task; it's a process. Conditions change continually, so risk management never ends. For that reason, I not only placed my story in a forest I knew well, but I also based it on my memories of a specific fire I helped fight when I was a boy. And though it happened a long time ago, I'll never forget that terrible scene —the charred tree trunks, the dead animals, the thick layer of ashes covering everything.

Now, almost fifty years later, anyone who walks through those woods sees nothing but green trees, lakes rippled by the wind, and land teeming with wildlife. It's as if nothing ever happened. But of course that's not true. Whenever a habitat, or a financial system, or a social system, takes that kind of blow, things are never really the same again.

Put another way, conditions around us change continually, and therefore so do the risks. Which means the only possible *constant* in life is the way you manage those risks—whether you're an individual investor, a business owner, or a corporate executive. Therefore, I hope this book helps you to begin creating a risk management approach you'll use for the rest of your life. Then, when you've carefully considered what you want, and what you need to do to get it, you'll be able to say with confidence: "I'll take *that* risk."

Acknowledgments

I would like to acknowledge: Walter Wriston, the gold standard of CEOs, who taught me the importance of ethics, good judgment, and reputational risk; John Reed, who taught me to think of market and enterprise risk in global terms; William Rhodes, who mentored me as I worked my way through the complexities of credit, sovereign, and counterparty risk; Lew Sanders, who taught me everything I know about investment risk; and Jerry Lieberman, the former president of Alliance-Bernstein, who opened my eyes to the importance of operational risk.

I would also like to thank the many talented people I had the privilege to work with throughout my career. There are truly too many of them to name.

Made in the USA
Charleston, SC
19 February 2014